D1716436

FLORIDA'S VANISHING ARCHITECTURE

Beth Dunlop

Photographs by Brian Smith

Florida's
Vanishing Architecture

Florida's Vanishing Architecture

Beth Dunlop

Photographs by Brian Smith

Pineapple Press, Inc.
Englewood, Florida

Library of Congress Cataloging-in-Publication Data

Dunlop, Beth, 1947-
    Florida's vanishing architecture.

    Series of articles that first appeared in the *Miami Herald*.
    Includes index.
    I. Architecture—Florida—Mutilation, defacement, etc.
2. Buildings—Florida—Remodeling for other use. I. *Miami
Herald* (Miami, Fla.) II. Title.
NA730.F6D8 1987   720'.9759   87-2433
ISBN 0-910923-39-6 (pbk.)

10 9 8 7 6 5 4 3 2 1

All of the essays in this book were originally printed in the
Miami Herald.

This book was in part made possible by the support of the
Friends of the Florida Endowment for the Humanities.

Printed by Kingsport Press, Kingsport, Tennessee

Design by Frank Cochrane Associates, Sarasota, Florida
Typography by Lubin Typesetting & Literary Services,
    Sarasota, Florida

This book is typeset in ITC Galliard, a contemporary adapta-
tion of Robert Granjon's sixteenth-century typeface design.
Mathew Carter created the contemporary version in 1978 for
Merganthaler Linotype.

Acknowledgments

My thanks to my editors, Doug Adrianson, Bill Greer, Kathy Martin, Ileana Oroza and Rhonda Prast for the nurture and attention they gave these essays; to Pete Weitzel, Heath Meriwether and Lou Heldman for affording me the time and freedom for this project. And thanks to those friends and colleagues who helped — John Rothchild, Sam Boldrick, George Percy, David Ferro, Walter Marder, Michael Zimney, Bill Thurston, Deana Primeles, Larry Paarlberg, Carl Abbott, Robert and Darryl Davis, and Al Burt. And to the University of Miami School of Architecture and the Florida South Chapter of the American Institute of Architects for making this book possible. And mostly, to Bill and Adam.

Contents

Introduction

Between the 20th of July and the 17th of August, 1986 the *Miami Herald* published a series of nine essays by its Pulitzer Prize nominee, Beth Dunlop, on the vanishing architecture of Florida. The essays carry the reader from Apalachicola to Key West, from De-Funiak Springs to Sarasota. They tell the tale of a Florida that in building its future is losing its past. It is a story of history being trampled, disfigured and disguised. It is a sentimental journey that takes us to pioneer days, to a less troubled past. It is a tale of naive tourism, of grand and elegant hotels filled with fantasy.

Her essays prompt the question: Where did Florida begin?

Some say Florida originated in a quest for a fountain of youth, others would argue that it started at a fort in St. Augustine which was built for no better reason than to keep the French at bay. Still others maintain that it began in a proud native Indian population that waged war against the European invaders until the 1840s and has never truly accepted defeat.

From the first incursion of the white-skinned for-eigners until almost the middle of the 19th century, misery and death characterized the history of Florida — the antithesis of the winter playground fantasy it represents to most people today. As recently as 1840, the Florida wilderness seemed indomitable except for a few isolated pockets of convalescence for the sick. But, except for the fort at St. Augustine, none of these people left traces in the form of buildings, or contributed to the state's architectural tradition.

Perhaps we should rephrase that question and ask, instead: Where does modern Florida begin?

Unlike the West, Florida was not born in gunfights and saloon showdowns but in freshwater springs and seasonal hotels. I would propose that modern Florida begins where fantasy overcomes circumstance. I would say that Florida began when one Alfred A. Lansing brought his camera to St. Augustine in 1842 and set about photographing its people, circuses and theatres. Photography had come to the United States only three years before, but already daguerreotypes were creating the stuff of the Florida dream with photos of the more picturesque sights from the border to Tal-lahassee, Apalachicola, and on down to Key West. Florida became — and remains — a state of visions to be mailed home. Would there be a Florida without a postcard and a snapshot?

One could argue that modern Florida only really began in 1842 when the steamer *St. Mathews* initiated weekly service between Savannah and Palatka and it became feasible for visitors to travel all the way from New York.

Or perhaps modern Florida was born in the railroad wars of the 1880s, when steamships, until then the only way to get here, were forced to give way to pas-senger trains with exotic names like the *Florida & West Indies Limited*, which could transport New Yorkers to Florida in just thirty-six hours.

Henry Morrison Flagler and Henry Bradley Plant, the two men most responsible for the development of modern Florida, were neither explorers nor politicians but railroad tycoons. Plant was an official of the Adams Express Company, responsible for its opera-

7

tions in the southeastern states. When a number of railroads in Florida and Georgia went bankrupt, Plant, with a few associates, bought controlling interest in some of them, and by 1882 had a line that extended into Florida. He recognized that to make his gamble successful, he had to provide not only transportation but also attractive destinations and accommodations for the tourists he was courting. Accordingly, he turned his considerable energies to developing Tampa and the string of towns along his routes, including St. Petersburg, Clearwater, and, appropriately, Plant City. To this end he built the Tampa Bay Hotel in 1888-91, and in 1904, the Belleview-Biltmore Hotel in Belleair.

Flagler came to St. Augustine in December, 1883. Hard on Plant's heels, Flagler bought the local rail line that ran from Jacksonville to St. Augustine, changed its name to the Florida East Coast Railway, and proceeded to extend it from New York down to Miami. Even before Plant began his Tampa Bay Hotel, Flagler was at work erecting the fabled Ponce de Leon Hotel in 1885, finished in 1888.

Plant and Flagler did not create the Florida resort hotel. Indeed, Flagler, who liked his comforts, might never have come to Florida at all had suitable accommodations not been available. Already the San Marco and the Villa Zorayda hotels of 1885 had introduced Moorish motifs into the evolving form of Florida architecture to compete with the gingerbread that characterizes the late Victorian era.

What both Plant and Flagler saw was that without an integrated system of railroads and gargantuan first-class hotels, Florida would remain a series of charming but isolated spots that would not pave the way for the statewide development and massive tourist industry they envisioned. The potential was so great that the two did not even feel obliged to compete. Flagler, in fact, was a major stockholder in some of Plant's companies, and there were interconnections between their two rail lines.

Meanwhile, designers of railroad cars were doing their best to match the standards set by the new luxury hotels, aided by the lurid copy of their advertising consultants. A Florida railroad booklet of 1887 promised that its "soft cushioned divans receive the body, a delicate luncheon is served at any hour. . . . they cannot be travellers. No, he is a guest on a hotel on wings!"

Modern Florida was built mainly by promoters and developers. The method is epitomized in the story of Palm Beach, a scruffy settlement of less than two dozen fairly primitive structures accessible only by boat that was transformed almost overnight into the posh retreat of millionaires, the very symbol of wealth and fashion.

Before 1899, the few determined visitors to Palm Beach arrived at Jupiter Inlet, the nearest steamship landing, and changed to a three-seat wagon drawn by two mules which jolted them overland for several miles to the west side of Lake Worth, where a ferry carried the exhausted travelers to Palm Beach. But in 1890 the opening of the so-called "celestial railway" (it stopped in Jupiter, Venus, Mars and Juno) allowed passengers to make only one change after arriving in Lake Worth. From there a small steamer paddled the remaining eight miles to Palm Beach. This improvement in access allowed Palm Beach to enjoy a rather peaceful period, but not for long. Flagler was busying himself with construction of a huge hotel — 540 rooms, no less, with a dining room to seat a thousand people! Flagler also began paving the streets and developing residential and commercial properties in the burgeoning resort. Within ten years, his already gigant hotel, the storied Royal Poinciana, doubled in size.

In spite of ups and downs, hurricanes and depression, the Palm Beach success story was repeated over and over again along the Florida east coast at various levels of splendor and success, transforming Florida from a war-torn, inaccessible wilderness into the promised land it seems to so many today in the most remarkable orgy of development the United States has ever witnessed.

The glamorous residents of Palm Beach, the glittering sands that Carl Fisher pumped onto mangrove swamp to make Miami Beach, the City Beautiful of Coral Gables that George Merrick created on his 3,000 acres of orange groves, and the hundreds of other resorts Florida promoters and developers are still constructing now do not constitute the whole of Florida, by any means. But they have suggested an architectural style for the state. Bound by no tradition, these developers have created a framework for fantasy, an illusion that begins in the late fall and lasts through the winter. Fishermen, ranchers, business people, and many others have their substantial Florida as well, and follow their own traditions and styles of building. As Beth Dunlop shows us in this series of essays, Florida architecture reflects them all: an enormous range that runs from the gossamer flamboyance of Disney World through the elegant classicism inherited from the Mediterranean, from the plantations of the antebellum South to the sturdy, practical simplicity of our fishing villages.

The challenge in these essays is for us to know and *use* our heritage. Our landmarks are not ivory towers, nor mummified corpses to be preserved and locked away for safekeeping. Like Vizcaya, they were mainly built for the delight of their original owners, but they survive only as long as they are visited and enjoyed. In her articles Beth Dunlop has begun to rediscover the road to the enjoyment of our architectural heritage. It is a path that begins at Key West and turns into a railway track through Miami, Palm Beach and St. Augustine, Tampa, Jacksonville and all those places that saw the light through Flagler's and Plant's trains. It is an avenue that remains vital today and must be rediscovered for a short and fragile history to survive and for our tradition to endure.

April 1987
Miami, Florida

José A. Gelabert-Navia
    Assistant Professor
    School of Architecture
    University of Miami

In Daytona Beach, the last small-scale hold-outs, cottages, survive in the midst of condominium development.

1

The Price of Progress

In building our future we are demolishing our past.

As rapidly as Florida is building its future, it is losing its past.

The two are not always cause and effect, but our lust for progress has driven us to trample much of our history — be it illustrious or ignominious or simply, and gloriously, commonplace.

We have neglected some of our greatest buildings to dereliction, altered others beyond recognition. Florida's architectural legacy is being threatened by forces that are rarely beyond our control, forces from age to avarice.

The pioneers who ventured into virgin oak hammocks or down untried streams built rugged and beautiful houses in sympathy with the land, and far

too many have been lost. Also gone are the homes of presidents, industrialists, literary giants.

Florida also lured those seeking a simple life in the sun, who settled into seaside villages and lakeside towns. The legacy of these fishermen and the orchard owners is just as much a part of Florida as the home of a Kennedy or a Rockefeller.

Also endangered are those subtle, small buildings and landscapes that add up to give Florida its persistent charm: quaint beach cottages; quirky old tourist attractions; fishing piers, where they have not already been demolished; lighthouses; "canopy" roads where the trees arch over the highway so beautifully.

In Florida, we can find landmarks of utopian quests

11

and towns that were planned to be ideal (Venice or Sebring), but those are disappearing, too; it is almost impossible to preserve anything as elusive as an idea expressed in architecture.

Too many vestiges of earlier industries are all but gone, from sugar mills to turpentine stills. The wonderful old shade barns where tobacco leaves were hung to dry have been carted away to become decks and den siding in suburban homes.

Only a few of the citrus packing houses remain, and the lumber industry's contribution can be explored inside a museum more easily than in an old mill town.

There are outlandishly elegant hotels, the cornerstones of even grander development schemes, and too many of them stand empty and deteriorating — giant relics of more glamorous days. We have enshrined those few remnants of the Spanish, English and French occupations of Florida, of the state's earliest settlements — essentially, its history before the 19th century. Yet there are cities in Florida — Miami, West Palm Beach and Jacksonville among them — where the more recent past has all but been wiped out. These 19th century buildings have fallen to fire and flood and hurricanes, but mostly to demolition.

Threats are legion

The threats to the state's architectural treasures are legion. The saga of a developer moving into a neighborhood and demolishing all the old buildings is typical; but the unexpected occurs almost as frequently. The 60-year-old Coliseum ballroom in St. Petersburg, where the movie *Cocoon* was filmed, is on the market. One reason is rising insurance rates.

Other threats include:

Decay: North of Tallahassee, the home of famous Florida carpetbagger Malachai Martin was ignored so long it eventually crumbled. It is still listed on the National Register of Historic Places; it is almost more difficult to get a building off the roll than onto it.

Inaction: Some of our finest landmarks sit derelict because their owners don't have the funds or the incentive to fix them up. The lyrical Freedom Tower in Miami sits decaying, as does the imposing San Carlos Hotel in Pensacola.

Acquisitiveness: Hospitals and universities are voracious devourers of old buildings. In St. Augustine, Flagler College, which occupies the spectacular Spanish-fantasy Ponce de Leon Hotel built by Henry Flagler in 1887, has just demolished two lovely Victorian houses across the street to build a new academic building.

Accident: In Miami, the exquisite 1916 Brown House slipped off a truck as it was being moved from its original location near the Omni (a hotel was planned for its site) to Watson Island. It sits there even now, one wing reduced to rubble. There is no money, public or private, for its repair.

Profit: "For Sale" signs stand in front of numerous historic properties, renowned or otherwise. It is Florida's continuing story. Anywhere that land can be assembled into marketable packages, the old buildings may be jeopardized.

Privacy: Legend has it that the heirs of Mrs. Potter Palmer, the bold Chicago millionairess who helped build Sarasota, matter-of-factly tore down her house, The Oaks, so it would not have another owner, ever.

Even tiny vestiges of Florida's past, the original Ybor City neon signs, are threatened.

Part of her property is now a historic site; part of it is an exclusive, walled subdivision.

And insensitivity: The Don Cesar in St. Petersburg Beach, long one of Florida's most marvelous hotels, is undergoing a renovation that will obliterate much of its old-fashioned appeal. In the end the Don Cesar's interior will look a lot like hundreds of other hotels — a Hilton or a Holiday Inn in a historic shell.

Sinners and saviors

Governments are both the sinners and the saviors here. The state Department of Transportation is particularly at fault: Its expansion policies have cost us a lot. Delightful little roadside buildings are sacrificed to highway-widening; graceful bridges are replaced by mammoth concrete spans. Some of our best panoramas of bay or sea have been blocked by insensitively designed roadway barriers.

Some local governments — a key example is Miami Beach — go so far as to demolish their own historic buildings, for reasons that are quite often truly trumped up. In just the past few years, a whole block of art deco buildings, a historic pine warehouse and a wonderful 60-year-old fishing pier, were torn down under city contracts.

Often, governments misjudge what is important to preserve. In Tampa, an ordinance is endangering the oversized neon signs — many of them 60 years old — in front of the theaters, clubs and casinos of Ybor City. These signs were not exempted as integral to the architecture of Tampa's historic Latin quarter when the city decided to clean up its other clutter.

On the other hand, no agency has worked harder to safeguard Florida's architectural treasures than the state's Bureau of Historic Preservation. And in counties and cities across Florida, preservation agencies are struggling to keep our history alive. Every year, more buildings are being listed on the National Register of Historic Places; more special districts are being named.

Saving buildings

In 1986, the Florida legislature voted a record $8.2 million to help save 24 important, endangered buildings.

Yet it is like the child's game of "Mother May I?" — one step forward and two steps back. For every building saved, for every neighborhood left intact, several more are threatened.

It is not a mass annihilation, not General Sherman's second sweep through the South. It is incremental, accidental — the gradual destruction of our heritage before too many of us had begun to know it.

And there is a rich heritage to know. Florida's history is vast and diverse, if not always flattering. It is in our architecture that we can see it, for architecture is the reflection of culture, the expression of our accomplishments.

We need our buildings to hold our memories for us: It is just that simple. Our architecture — be it houses or churches or whole cities — stores history, definitively, in a way that no library can. In our buildings, we can reach out and touch history.

To lose Florida's historic architecture, either willfully or unwittingly, would be to lose our past. We can't afford that.

A fleet of 200 sponge-fishing boats once worked out of Tarpon Springs.

2

From Fishing Villages to Tourist Traps

We crush fragile fishing villages, then have to settle for nostalgia because there is so little else left.

The fishermen who settled in Florida came from Nantucket and the shores of North Carolina, and they brought along the architectural traditions of other places and other times. They settled in villages tucked away along the coast, and they filled their towns with hand-hewn cottages and extravagant, filigreed houses.

These were picturesque places without pretensions, and some have survived a century or more. We know them as Fernandina, Cedar Key, Apalachicola, Cortez, Key West. Even their names evoke images of weathered wood and tin roofs, of widow's walks and ornate porches, of battered boats snugged into the harbor and the day's catch on display.

But where once fishermen dried their nets, suburban shoppers now price macrame. High-priced yachts fill marinas where only hard-working fishing boats used to dock. Processing plants have given way to restaurants, and weather-beaten neighborhoods sport new coats of bright paint.

Florida's fishing villages have become chic little clusters of boutiques, coveted residential resorts, trendy tourist destinations. Their appeal is irresistible, and almost unwittingly we have all but wiped them out.

The story here is, of course, of money — intertwined tales of once-innocent places succumbing to the diverse temptations of the times.

The canny fishermen of a century ago chose prized

Part of the old Tarpon Springs Sponge Exchange, right, where sponge-divers once auctioned their booty, was torn down to build the new sponge exchange, left, which sells frozen yogurt and "Miami Vice" T-shirts.

locations — sheltered harbors with warm waters, islands already photogenic. Their villages survived for generations, through boom and bust.

Times change: The big conglomerates have made the independent fishing industry falter. And those same sheltered coves that originally lured fishermen provide safe landing for smuggled drugs, a haven for recreational boats, perfect backdrops for Instamatic snapshots and glossy postcard views that draw the people in.

Changing Cortez

Drive toward Cortez, a generations-old fishing village nestled into Sarasota Bay and surrounded by Bradenton, and its future seems inevitable: The six-lane highways, routes 41 and 684, are lined with signs of the times — a mind-numbing array of gas stations, fast food outlets, shopping centers, auto dealers. New construction lines the highways: Villages at Lakeside, Main Street at Lakeside, Shorewalk, Pinebrook Commons, Cortez Commons.

The road narrows and then there is Cortez.

On one side of the highway the village remains much as it has all this century, population 500: white cottages with laundry hanging outside, the old packing houses, a volunteer fire department. It is quiet, self-possessed, mundane — with no nod to worldliness except a franchise lobster ''shanty'' restaurant.

But on the other side of the highway a new world has swallowed up the old. There are restaurants, marinas, tour boats, apartment buildings. As Cortez disappears it is being replaced by condominiums with nautical names — Mariners Cove and, not without a bit of irony, Smugglers Landing — so its beginnings will at least be remembered.

Sometimes development comes in a swoop, as it has at Cortez. Other times it seems to sneak in. Travel the length of Pine Island, tucked between Fort Myers and Sanibel. Long sparsely populated except for the fishermen who settled in the tiny towns of Bokeelia, Matlacha and St. James City, now it is dotted with little developments, and slowly but surely the island is burgeoning.

Key West drew in newcomers over the years; now it is being overwhelmed. Fernandina, long a showplace of caring restoration, faces the incursion of new industry and, with it, new residents. The rest — shops, offices, motels, condominiums — is sure to follow.

It is expected, probably even unavoidable, but the nature of change is nonetheless shocking. When places formerly so chaste become commercialized, the juxtapositions can be jarring.

Wanting too much

At Cedar Key, midway between Tampa and the Panhandle, lunch at the waterfront is $9.95 and up. On the pier, tourists fish. The harbor promenade is spilling over with shops selling ceramics and silkscreened shirts, there to be bought by the occupants of the new tin-roofed two-story condos and motels that march around the island's circumference.

Cedar Key was a sizable lumber shipping port and pencil manufacturing center in the 19th century that was bypassed by the cross-Florida railroad in 1886 and then virtually destroyed by a hurricane in 1896. For most of this century, the population hovered at 900.

It was a quaint and enchanting place, an unreconstructed 19th century town with its requisite complement of artists and writers, along with mullet fishermen.

Tourists have always trekked the 22 miles off U.S. 98 and across the causeway to enjoy Cedar Key's eccentricities. The island also hosted two annual festivals, one art and one seafood. In the last decade or so, these events began to draw up to 100,000 — popularity that spelled Cedar Key's doom.

Cedar Key, once sleepy and inaccessible, gained popularity through its annual seafood festival. What followed was rapid growth that undermined much of what the old fishing key had to offer. Photographs by Allen Freeman.

In the Gulf Coast fishing village of Cortez, one side of the highway remains much as it was in this old photo. The other side of the highway now sports restaurants and condos with nautical names. Photograph courtesy of Florida State Archives.

There never was a nefarious scheme at work here, just people wanting too much of a vulnerable place. We crush these fragile fishing villages, by design or by accident, or let them languish, and then we have to settle for nostalgia because there is so little else left. The irony is that festivals such as Cedar Key's end up celebrating more what is already gone than what is still there.

All over America, fake fishing villages that lure more tourists than fish are being built along the waterfront — in Baltimore and Norfolk and Toledo, among other places. Florida is getting its fair share, from Tin City in Naples to the ambitious Bayside in Miami.

Punta Gorda, overlooking Charlotte Harbor near the mouth of the Peace River, has an ersatz fisherman's village just down the street from the town, which is a real fisherman's village with charming if shabby tin-roofed cottages.

A half-century ago, Punta Gorda's pier was called, rather inelegantly, the City Fish Docks, but fire demolished the buildings there. Eventually, Punta Gorda's fishing industry lost its momentum, and developers sought a new use for the old dock.

The commercial Fisherman's Village is clad in imitation weathered wood — a two-story complex with shops on the ground floor and time-sharing apartments upstairs. Visitors stroll past knick-knack and clothing shops; their parked cars get a good view of the marina.

The sponge exchange

Tarpon Springs, a Greek-settled town that evolved from sponge diving center to tourist trap, has long had a kind of corny appeal. Along its historic wharf a ''museum'' offers a three-dimensional history of the sponge industry; the ''Spongearama'' tells the tale in a multimedia version. Hawkers peddle their wares — sponges, loofahs, trinkets — from behind Corinthian columns, and loudspeakers announce, for the town to hear, the departure of sponge-diving boat rides.

But somewhere along the way, all this was deemed not to be enticing enough to today's tourist. The new Tarpon Springs Sponge Exchange is a crisp white, blue-trimmed Bauhaus-styled building, where exotic flavors of frozen yogurt and *Miami Vice* T-shirts are on sale — a sponge exchange in name only. Where it stands was for years the old sponge exchange, the real one, a rambling row of ''cells'' where the fishermen cleaned and auctioned off their diving haul. A developer tore down all but a half-dozen of the cells and built a shopping mall. It is very tasteful, very restrained and entirely out of place in this tacky touristy town.

We little cherish the sweetness, the humor, the workaday charm of what we have. This is an age of exploitation, an era where marketing slogans reign over reality. We cannot seem to leave things alone.

The sadness is that our children will not partake of the heritage of the American independent fisherman; they will not know the beguiling brusqueness of a fishing village at work, for all they will ever see is the adulterated version. ''And is that the restaurant over there?'' asked my 3-year-old son, gazing at a picture of a harbor in a children's book.

Once — and not too long ago — fishing villages were for fishing.

The houses of Apalachicola are testament to the town's prosperous past as a cotton and milled-wood shipping port.

3

Apalachicola – Florida's Living Museum

In many ways, this village is Florida's last chance to retain a piece of its past, a real one rather than a simulation.

A century ago, Apalachicola was a thriving town — a cotton shipping port and a fishing village. It grew and it flourished. Mill owners, merchant shippers and seafarers built grand manses with vast porches and rooftop lookouts, perched proudly on the bluff overlooking the bay.

Oh, there were modest enterprises as well, and modest houses — tin-roofed wood cottages with tiny, elegant porches. They were an evidence of aspirations. The 19th century was filled with promise for Apalachicola: cotton shipping, lumber and wood novelty works, net manufacturing and fishing.

But the promise of one century is not always fulfilled in the next, and as the railroads took over for shipping and the big mills replaced the small ones, Apalachicola was left behind.

Buffeted by hurricanes and plagued by poverty, it nonetheless endured, almost untouched by modern times. The houses of the successful seamen remain, still splendid, still stately. So do the humble cottages. The churches, the commercial buildings, the packing houses all emanate from an era past. It is eerie, in a way, and exulting in another, to see that time really has stood still here.

'A living museum'

Apalachicola is a breathtaking place, an extraordinary town filled with extraordinary architecture, from

25

An Apalachicola country house falls quietly into disrepair.

the simple 1836 Sponge Exchange — Florida's first —
to its magnificent Victorian houses, from its rundown
waterfront to its impeccable churches.

"It is a museum, a living museum," says David
Ferro, chief architect for the state's Bureau of Historic
Preservation.

Apalachicola is also at a crossroads: It cannot survive
as it is, a population dependent on the vagaries of a
seasonal oyster industry. It is very poor.

In town, the shambles of the economy are evident.
Far too many houses are tumble-down, in need of
paint or repairs. On Market Street, little shopping
is being done. Only the Gibson Inn — refurbished
beautifully and reopened just last fall as a Victorian
town hotel — stands in testimony to hope for a richer
future.

But all along the Panhandle, the steady march of
condominiums toward Apalachicola is a reality. Across
the bay, St. George Island is filling up; for two years,
developers have been petitioning Franklin County,
unsuccessfully so far, to be allowed to build marinas in
Apalachicola Bay, the source of the area's primary
livelihood, oysters.

The Reverend Tom Weller perches on the porch of an Episcopal rectory, built in 1900.

The threats to Apalachicola are twin ones — poverty and prosperity. Without economic growth, it could become a near ghost town. With affluence, it could lose its authenticity, and who can put a price on that?

The confounding problem here is to revive Apalachicola without ruining it, to let the town flourish once again without destroying the remarkable legacy of its architecture, of its industry, of its populace. The easiest answers — short-term solutions such as building condominiums in the harbor or luring light industry — would spell doom for this untrammeled town.

School for restoration

Apalachicola is not without its angels. Florida A&M University, in conjunction with three state agencies — historic preservation, environmental regulation and education — is planning to open a school for restoration crafts, an institute to train the grandchildren of the woodworkers who produced the cornices and balusters and filigree trim of the ornate houses. It is an effort to build additional resources without having to lure large-scale industry.

Joey Taranto and son Anthony show off freshly-caught mullet outside their family-owned business in Apalachicola.

More ambitious, and more visionary, is a plan to have the state buy the wharf area under the Conservation and Recreation Land Program (CARL), a program more often used for virgin hammocks or unspoiled beachfront land. The idea is to create a ''working waterfront,'' to let Apalachicola become, formally, a museum without walls; visitors would be able to see the day's catch being brought in, fish and oysters being cleaned, nets being made or repaired — without corniness or contrivance.

Executed with dignity, it could be brilliant — a public appreciation of skills and crafts we have almost lost.

In many ways, Apalachicola is Florida's last chance to retain a piece of its past, a real one rather than a simulation. Today, Apalachicola is untainted. If we destroy it, we'll never get it back.

A dinosaur houses Harold's Auto Center near Weeki Wachee. It may have to be demolished if the state widens U.S. 19.

4

Roadside Architecture – Last Relics of Early Tourism

Not all of the offerings were great or even good architecture, but added up, the fragments of old Florida turned it into a special place.

Once, Florida was a place to be savored up close. Poets and pundits extolled its graces: tropical gardens, burbling springs, beguiling towns. The pace was slow, the offerings intimate.

This was the uncelebrated Florida, the Florida of mom 'n' pop motels carefully landscaped with trellis roses or camelias. It was the Florida of "Goofy Golf" courses, of hand-built restaurants serving home cooking.

And the tourists came — by boat, by train, by car and even in their "tin can" trailers. They got gas at Hansel-and-Gretel houses or from service stations shaped like giant dinosaurs; they gazed at alligators or flamingos or parrots performing tricks, and they gloried in the natural beauty of the land and water.

Florida was amazing, offbeat, enchanting. From the start, the impulse to show off African monkeys or Brazilian parrots in a near-tropical setting was irresistible. It wasn't so much creating another world — bringing Morocco or Paris to Tampa or Orlando the way Busch and Disney did much later — as luxuriating in the world that was already there.

If, on the jungle cruises that decades later still explore Florida's rivers, the animals were imported, at least they were real animals. At Disney World today, the bears are bionic, the elephants automated, the bird calls piped in.

And if the main building at Weeki Wachee Springs

north of St. Petersburg was styled after a Russian hunting lodge, so be it; it was done with every intent of creating something beautiful, and at least it wasn't a franchise. Tourists to Weeki Wachee now stay in a Holiday Inn just across the speeding U.S. 19 traffic.

The advertisements were seductive. At Rainbow Springs there were "434 acres of heavily wooded land into which thousands of exotic and unusual flowers, plants, ferns and palms have been introduced, threaded through with charming paths. One of the most interesting sights is Rainbow Falls . . . which plunges 53 feet over cliffs framed by dense tropic vegetation into a beautiful rock garden and fernery below."

The lodge there was built in 1938 of wood and stone; the cottages, for rent ($7.50-to-$9 a night) and open year-round, were quaint creations of rustic style. At the end of the Depression, there was a rainbow to offer a respite.

Winter cottages now stand deserted in Parker, in the Florida Panha

Today, stern "No Trespassing" signs warn visitors away. Rainbow Springs has been turned into a sprawling subdivision, carved out of the gently rolling hills north of Dunellon. The cottages, once prime tourist accommodations, now house the development's "shipping and receiving" and utilities departments.

For a century, Florida's springs (it has 27 top-quality freshwater springs, more than in any other state) were a major inducement. They drew in the visitors with their rapid-flowing, crystal-clear waters, home to brilliant-hued fish and perfect for boating, swimming, sightseeing and even restorative cures.

But tourists speed past them these days, barely bothering to take the five-minute detour off the highway to see the manatees or feed the squirrels at Homosassa Springs, one of the prettiest and most ecologically interesting of Florida's springs, saved from its financial problems two years ago when Citrus County bought it.

Public ownership seems to be the best way to keep all of these old attractions from going the way of Silver Springs or even Weeki Wachee, where you walk past four gift shops before you see the first natural sight. The simple pleasures of Florida's past are just not profitable, especially when pitted against Magic Kingdoms. At the very least, they must have a water slide.

State and springs

The state will become the full owner of Wakulla Springs near Tallahassee in November, offering hope that this — the least-altered of any of Florida's operating springs — will give us a glimpse of nature as the early tourists saw it. The lodge at Wakulla, built by financier Edward Ball as a private guest house, has retained much of its original eccentric character — diminished only by a new bright-orange roof over the lodge's porch and a ticket sales building that looks like a Sunoco station.

The springs of Florida offer a sharp lesson in history, for once they shared many similarities: a rustic lodge, a rather elegant bath house, a glass-bottom boat. Now they offer only contrasts — from the abandoned bath house of Suwanee Springs, which sits in the North Florida woods to be seen only by canoeists and hikers, to the vast, overblown commercialization of Silver Springs.

Admittedly, not all of the offerings were great or even good architecture. But added up, the fragments

of old Florida turned it into a truly special place.

We've lost much of it to the developer's wrecking ball and the interstate-highway steamrollers. The size of our buildings and the pace of our lives are much different from what they were in the 1950s.

Along the roads

The roadside lures of miniature golf or drive-in restaurants can't capture an audience from I-75. Just last year, an original "Goofy Golf" was dismantled in West Palm Beach, and the bizarre zoo creatures were sunk in the ocean to create one of the strangest snorkel spots ever. The new miniature golf courses — and almost the only place where they are still being built is on Panama City's weird and wonderful Miracle Mile, a mind-boggling ode to the honky-tonk — are really macro-miniature golf with waterfalls and volcanoes.

Drive-in restaurants and gas stations in all sorts of strange configurations — castles, cabins, creatures — used to line our roadways; now they have virtually vanished. And even the last holdouts are endangered: The dinosaur that houses Harold's Auto Service may have to be demolished if the state widens U.S. 19 from six to eight lanes north of New Port Richey.

Too, the mom 'n' pop motels and colonies of cottages — tiny, unpretentious enclaves called Piney Nook Beach or Sun Glow or Salt Air or Cozy Cottages — are imperiled in a place where hotels build pools covering acres. This is not to say that they'll disappear; they won't. But the tiny beachfront cottage is already an exception along Florida's 1,300 miles of coastline.

The survivors are few: On Grayton Beach, long a cluster of simple beachfront houses in the Panhandle, almost every lot is being filled. "For Sale" signs line the road along Englewood's Manasota Key beaches. On Fort Myers Beach, the cottages cluster together, like refugees from a storm; the condominiums — Kiwi, Kahlua, Lahaina, Lani Kai — are taking over.

The age of bland

The Florida of today is homogenized, pasteurized, purified. The new condominiums of Fort Myers may all have Hawaiian-sounding names, but their design is continental-American bland. In Miami, on Sunny Isles' "Motel Row," the Chinese-Polynesian-styled Castaways Hotel was destroyed last year to make way for some utterly banal high-rise condominiums; the Castaways was perhaps the most outstanding example

"Mom and Pop" motels, such as the Spanish Courts, were intimate and designed with personal flair. In Florida, few remain. Photographs by William Farkas.

On the road to Ocala, a jumble of signs tells the story of Florida's rapid growth. Allen Freeman

of kooky architecture in Florida, and its loss was tragic.

It's just one example, though. On Motel Row and all over Florida, the relaxed, genial, even silly architecture is being wiped away. In its place we are getting buildings that are too tall, too fat, too boring and much too uptight.

This is not mere lament. Surely Florida will never look the same viewed at high speed and huge scale; it will be a blur punctuated by condo gatehouses and golden arches. But there is more to it than that. The social and political implications of our allowing the small stuff to disappear are profound: The day is not far away when those of moderate income will find it impossible to stay on the beach or visit most of the state's attractions. Florida ought not become a privilege of income.

As much as anything, this is a matter of public policy. Change is on its way anywhere the zoning allows for greater density — on the beaches, the bays and even inland. It's like dominoes: Once the people come to fill the new buildings, the roads must be widened to accommodate their cars; next to go are the funky old gas stations or the idiosyncratic little roadside restaurants.

Hokey, tender, even foolish — it all gave Florida a special charm. When we lose it, we'll lose a lot.

The vacant and vandalized John Ringling Towers was called the "Aristocrat of Beauty" when it opened in 1926 as the El Vernona. In 1983, a permit was issued for its demolition.

5

The Grand Old Hotels – Fading Fantasies

Problems ranging from structural deterioration to financial insolvency threaten once-great hotels.

The Hotel San Carlos stands silent sentinel over Pensacola, dominating the city's skyline and its psyche. The doors are locked, the windows barricaded. Inside, the furniture — the overstuffed chairs where generations of visitors lounged — gathers dust.

Once it was the best destination in a glamorous old city. Once it was Pensacola's centerpiece.

For almost a century, Florida's grand hotels held court in formidable style. Duchesses and dowagers arrived for a week or a season, and if you weren't royal or rich, you could pretend to be. You could dine in a medieval banquet hall, dance in a Renaissance courtyard. And if it wasn't a real Renaissance courtyard, so

be it; it was all there for the imagining.

In a grand hotel, you could live your finest fantasies. In a grand hotel, you could dream.

But fantasies fade and dreams die: It is a terrible truth of time. Today, far too many of these hotels stand decaying and decrepit — sober, moldering reminders of gala days gone by.

For Pensacola, the San Carlos, though now empty, is a repository of rich memories, a vacant reminder that the city no longer prospers the way it once did.

A visitor in 1916, four years after the hotel opened, wrote home about it this way:

"It is known as the San Carlos and has a slightly Waldorfian manner, going in rather too extravagantly for marble pillars, palms, gold and gilt, steam heat, page boys, telephone girls, lounges, cigar stands, express elevators and sky-scraper proportions. It did not seem possible that there could be a great enough floating population in Pensacola to warrant the magnificence of the hotel.''

That was the amazement of it all. In Florida, where alligators crawled and 'possums prowled, a hotel so splendid was an anomaly; this wasn't Paris, after all, or Madrid or Rome.

Yet at the Tampa Bay Hotel, you could sit in a sofa that was once Marie Antoinette's. In St. Petersburg, the hotelier Aymer Laughner put Pompeiian murals on the dining hall walls in the striking bay-front Vinoy Park Hotel.

For the Ponce de Leon Hotel in St. Augustine, Henry Flagler chose a young decorator who would furnish window carvings, paintings and chandeliers — and design some stained-glass windows for it as well. His name: Louis Comfort Tiffany.

The architects — some as famous as Stanford White or the firm of Carrere and Hastings, others little-known — made certain their buildings would be memorable. They built Italian palazzi, Moorish fortresses, Spanish castles or French chateaus; they painted them peach or yellow or pink, as the Don Cesar was so boldly on St. Petersburg Beach.

With turrets and minarets and spires silhouetted against the sky, the hotels cast a magic spell. Across the flat Miami landscape, the wedding-cake filigree tower of the Coral Gables Biltmore beckoned. The twin towers of the Breakers rose above the royal palms to etch out the townscape of Palm Beach.

They were imposing, flamboyant, posh. The ballrooms were stage sets for extravaganzas; the dining rooms more sumptuous than the food.

A few hotels — most notably the Breakers in Palm Beach and the Boca Raton Hotel and Club — have never been allowed to decline. Others — the Belleview Biltmore in Belleair, near Clearwater, the Casa Marina in Key West and the Crown Hotel in Inverness — have been renovated and reach back to another era's glory. The Coral Gables Biltmore is undergoing a painstaking restoration that will return it to its original luster.

But they are the happy exceptions; too many of our grand hotels have ended up abandoned hulks with peeling paint and broken windows. Winos sleep where Paul Whiteman's orchestra used to play; rats scurry across derelict dining rooms.

The exterior of the Don Cesar in St. Petersburg Beach still is a dazzler. The interior, however, is changing.

Barbed wire tops the chain-link fence that protects St. Petersburg's 62-year-old Vinoy Park Hotel from trespassers. The hotel is now half-renovated: Outside it sports a new coat of burnt-peach paint; inside, it is still the empty, vandalized shell it has been for years.

Since 1974, developers have tried to find a new use for the Vinoy Park and failed. One potential operator auctioned off all the handmade dark gray, walnut-inlaid furniture and leather and wrought-iron sconces and chandeliers. Another proposed surrounding the seven-story hotel with high-rise condominiums; he lost a court fight with preservationists. And so the Vinoy Park sits, awaiting a new use, a new life.

In Sarasota, the massive, hulking John Ringling Towers hovers over Route 41, vacant and vandalized. When it opened, in 1926, it was called the El Vernona, and its sloganeers called it "Aristocrat of Beauty." Its entrance was paved with tiles from Seville; carved wood from Spanish galleons adorned the lobby. In 1983, its owners obtained a demolition permit, but the bulldozers have yet to arrive.

The urban hotels pose particular problems. John Ringling Towers, for example, stands perilously close to Route 41 and its congested traffic. A future as a hotel or apartments is hard to envision; other alternatives are even more elusive. So too at Pensacola's San Carlos, which is sandwiched in on all sides. One problem it faces is limited parking.

The Biscaya, overrun with cats and cockroaches, has been a symbolic gateway to Miami Beach since the hotel was built in 1924; these days it marks as much as anything a city's falling fortunes. It is the sole survivor of Miami Beach's boom years, and it is caught in a web of complications.

The city ordered the Biscaya's demolition, but the owner fought that order in court and won a delay. Still, little is happening. Both the owner and a prospective buyer have eyes on the Biscaya's renovation, but no one has the financing to restore it.

The Ormond Beach Hotel sprawls along the Halifax River, the biggest wood-frame structure in America and one of Florida's oldest hotels. It dates back to 1887. At the turn of the century, it was an important winter resort, a destination for America's elite; today it is part retirement home, part bed-and-breakfast.

The Ormond was allowed to deteriorate so much that it faces multimillion-dollar renovation costs — depending on the extent of the refurbishment.

St. Petersburg's 62-year-old Vinoy Park Hotel sports a new coat of paint, but inside it is still a vandalized shell.

The Hotel Ormond, once one of Florida's grandest, has been allowed to deteriorate badly over the years. Photograph courtesy of Florida State Archives.

Though there is a new restaurant in the lobby, mostly it is a musty and shabby place, a time-worn relic of a more luxurious era.

The decades have discovered a panoply of new uses for these old places; some have become flop houses, barracks, even banks.

Others have become colleges. The elegant Spanish Rolyat, built in the St. Petersburg neighborhood of Gulf Shores, is now Stetson Law School. The Tampa Bay Hotel — a minaret-topped Moorish masterpiece built in 1891 and one of the most spectacular buildings in Florida — has become the University of Tampa. In St. Augustine, the gorgeous 99-year-old Ponce de Leon — all spires and steps and formal passageways — is now Flagler College, and is easily the most stunning structure in a city full of marvelous buildings.

There is an uneasy balance between the academic and the historic in these hotels-turned-universities. At the University of Tampa notices of schedule changes are taped on marble columns. The bathrooms have been "modernized" — enough so that the main-floor ladies' room sports condo-contemporary colors of lime green and white. In the once-opulent ballroom, students sit in red plastic chairs and take notes.

Still other hotels have been subjected to humiliating renovations that have virtually wiped out their historic character. The Don Cesar on St. Petersburg Beach is an example. Built in 1928, it was always a dazzler — rough, rustic and romantic. This summer, it is being renovated in an appalling manner: The old multi-pane windows that shimmered like diamonds in the sunlight are being ripped out to make way for ordinary double-hung ones; the swirled stucco walls are being sanded down and covered with silk-patterned vinyl wallpaper, and the rooms are being furnished with copies of French country furniture.

It is all very synthetic, and it is all very sad.

The problems Florida's great old hotels face range from structural deterioration to financial insolvency. Decades of sorry neglect have taken their toll.

And yet, even in abandonment the grand old hotels capture our fantasies in stone and stucco. They are a metaphor for our best hopes and worst fears. They hold the promise that we'll somehow not let past grandeur disappear, and the fear, too, that in the end we'll succumb to the bland realities of modern life.

We can't afford to lose them — they're far too beautiful, far too important, to let go — and we can't afford to keep them. It's a tormenting situation.

The Palmettos, built in 1877, overlooking the St. Johns River, is empty, inaccessible and for sale.

6

Homes of the Famous – Who Owns History?

Sometimes the houses were more illustrious than their owners; sometimes it was the other way around.

High on a hill in the dense Central Florida woods is a historic house constructed by ship's carpenters in 1849 of hand-hewn timbers. It was called Chinsegut Hill by the retired colonel who owned it for many decades. Once it was open to view, but no more. Now Chinsegut Hill is a university's secluded domain, and uninvited guests are not welcome.

Nor can visitors poke around the spooky Victorian chambers of The Palmettos, built in 1877 on a bluff overlooking the St. Johns River in a settlement called Fort Gates. It is empty, inaccessible and for sale. Stern warnings and guard dogs keep trespassers off The Palmettos' grounds.

No "For Sale" sign ever stood in front of Spottis Woode, a lush Tudor-style mansion perched above Clearwater Harbor, where Donald Roebling, great-grandson of the builder of the Brooklyn Bridge and an inventor himself, once lived. But Spottis Woode just sold for $1.5 million, passing without fanfare from private hands to private hands.

The renowned and the rich came to Florida and erected extravagant, eloquent houses. Sometimes the houses were more illustrious than their owners; sometimes it was the other way around. Presidents, power-brokers and poets all settled here, yet we little commemorate their presence.

Even when such houses do fall into the public realm

Stately trees shade the secluded grounds at Chinsegut Hill in central Florida.

we often treat them cavalierly, abusing their architecture, trifling with tradition, ignoring the accomplishments of their occupants. Where a story could be told, we shun it. Where there is a tale to unfold, we avoid it.

No other aspect of preservation is as tricky as this, admittedly. The fate of the houses of the rich and famous poses questions political, philosophical and fiscal. The conflict between privacy and history is nowhere stronger. After all, who owns history?

Of course, the past is mostly preserved in battlefields and legislative chambers, in declarations of war and treaties of peace. But when we want to know the people behind the dramas and the documents, we should be able to look at where they lived — and how.

In Palm Beach, the family of the late President John F. Kennedy convinced the Town Council that their home, where Kennedy spent his winter vacations, wasn't even a local landmark, let alone a candidate for the National Register of Historic Places. Richard Nixon's Key Biscayne compound was drastically altered before anyone got a chance to decide whether it just might have some historic value. Still, in Key West, we do have Harry Truman's "winter White House," and a Methodist children's home in Sanford still owns a bed in which Grover Cleveland slept.

In an ideal world, we would turn our most renowned houses into museums, open to visitors, as so many of the great and wonderful houses of Europe are. Instead they sit, unheralded either for their exquisite architecture or important history, when either should be enough to warrant our attention.

Pragmatically, we don't have the mechanisms to acquire even the most significant of houses; were there legislative means, there wouldn't be the money anyway. The price tags for vast villas are exorbitant these days.

Just last year, Dade County and the state of Florida scrambled to come up with $22.5 million to buy Charles Deering's vast Cutler homestead, and that included 380 acres of rare woods. When Marjorie Meriwether Post left two homes — including her extraordinary Palm Beach mansion, Mar-a-Lago — to the federal government, it turned down the gift, saying the upkeep would be impossibly expensive. Eventually, developer Donald Trump bought Mar-a-Lago for more than $7 million.

Post's gift, though thwarted, was an exception. This is an era when estates go on the auction block for astronomical sums; only rarely do philanthropic families bequeath their homes to the public.

This is more typical: Epping Forest, the lavish Spanish-style estate of Alfred I. duPont in Jacksonville, is being turned into a yacht club as part of an exclusive housing development. The Mediterranean home of William K. Vanderbilt on Fisher Island in Miami's Government Cut is being restored as an exclusive restaurant for the island's residents and guests.

The Casa de Josefina, a medieval Spanish castle

built just south of Lake Wales in 1925 by an Indiana-born developer, was on its way to becoming a club-house for La Casa Condos. But the condominium development was never finished, so the sprawling old castle was returned to private ownership; its gardens and grounds are gone and the house simply sits there, perched awkwardly in front of rows of garden apartments.

Public ownership by itself isn't the only answer; the legacy of the architecture and the integrity of the past must be safeguarded as well.

Vizcaya, the museum that was James Deering's Northern Italian palazzo on Biscayne Bay, is undergoing an appalling change: Its courtyard is being enclosed under a futuristic glass pyramid roof, allowing for central air-conditioning. It might save the furniture, but it will ruin the architecture, and at Vizcaya, the architecture is far superior.

John D. Rockefeller spent 13 winters in Ormond Beach in a severe-looking Victorian house he called The Casements. To see it now, you'd never know it.

Arts and crafts — quilts, carvings, ceramics — are displayed in empty downstairs rooms. An elegant dining loggia with graceful arched windows, French doors and a fireplace was stripped of all its amenities to make a windowless room with ceiling fans and track lights.

On the second floor, one bedroom houses a collection of Hungarian crafts; the top floor is given over to a display of Boy Scout memorabilia.

Floors have been clad in linoleum tile, ceilings sheathed in Styrofoam popcorn or acoustic tile. Where there used to be a Tiffany skylight, there is now clear glass with colored spotlights aimed at it.

The Casements is operated as a cultural center by Ormond Beach. After Rockefeller's death in 1937, it became a nursing home, then stood vacant and vandalized for years before the city bought it. Somehow, that doesn't make up for the fact that there is virtually no nod to the house's former role. It could be any house.

Oddly, in Florida we obliterate legacies of great consequence, then celebrate the past where there is little to regard. At Eden Gardens near Point Washington in

John D. Rockefeller spent 13 winters in The Casements, now a cultural center in Ormond Beach.

the Panhandle, the state's Department of Natural Resources runs tours through a century-old mill owner's house that was bought, drastically altered and decorated by a New York journalist during the 1960s. She closed in porches, added vinyl tile to floors, installed central air-conditioning and furnished it with her own antiques.

Eden Gardens may be amusing, even attractive, but it is hardly history. Real history is made by those who wanted to change the world — through wealth or wits or wisdom. We learn it reading; we learn it looking.

In Florida, that history, as showcased in the homes of people who made an impact, is slipping away from us before we can even learn it.

This Cross Creek cottage was Marjorie Kinnan Rawlings' "small place of enchantment."

7

Cross Creek – A Survivor Amid the Subdivisions

Beauty still reigns at Marjorie Kinnan Rawlings' "place of enchantment" despite growth and development.

"I do not understand how anyone can live without some small place of enchantment to turn to," wrote Marjorie Kinnan Rawlings in her memoirs.

From 1928 to 1941, Rawlings lived in Cross Creek in peaceful communion with the land. Her enthralling, reverential prose came from the tranquil existence she found in this remote and beautiful place in the woods and orange groves of North Florida. At a typewriter on her front porch, she wrote remarkable stories of backwoods Florida life, including her most famous novel, *The Yearling*.

In those years, she learned to endure the hardships of the winter and appreciate the forced indolence of the summer. She was city bred, so it was an adventure at first; eventually Cross Creek became a passion, an obsession.

Still today, it is an inconspicuous spot, miles off the main roads, past the fishing camps and the small lodges and over the bridge. But a steady stream of tourists pulls up in front of the home of one of Florida's most famous writers.

In truth, there's not much to learn when the park ranger gives a guided tour of the unadorned cracker house, simply furnished. The insights it could offer are too subtle to be gleaned in a half-hour visit.

Once Cross Creek was merely an out-of-the-way destination for literary pilgrims. But when Rawlings' memoirs were turned into a movie called *Cross Creek* and filmed there as well, the alluring images of the place put it on the tourist map.

The movie put Cross Creek in the center of controversy as well. Tourism picked up, and suddenly every available acre sported a subdivision sign. The biggest landholder, the Owens Illinois Corp., planned a 29,000-unit development. Another landowner proposed a 500-space recreational vehicle park. It was all very scary.

Fly over Florida, and you will see vast acres of empty green grass, trees, lakes. But drive through the state and you will see that the land is accounted for. The subdividers have staked their claims.

"Heritage Log Homes — Country Lifestyle Inc." announces one such sign, as if it were possible to become an instant pioneer by moving just east of the little towns of Bishopville and Barberville on State Route 40.

The paradox is powerful: As we create such rustic communities on half-acre — or even five-acre — plots, we are endangering the real rural towns. They are threatened by growth and development and by commercialism and tourism.

Retirees seeking quieter lives have fled the urbanized coasts for the inland hills. Corporations seeking a mild climate and easy living for employees have found their spots as well. Draw a line from Orlando to Gainesville and another from Tampa to Gainesville, and you will track Florida's new growth.

In many of Florida's rural counties, the population has doubled in a decade and that rate of growth is increasing. And even if it may not seem like much in actual numbers, the impact is profound. Between 1980 and 1985, Ocala — the place where those two lines converge on the map — charted the nation's third-largest proportionate population growth, a 32.3 percent increase.

For Florida's sleepy inland towns, Ocala or Micanopy or Melrose, and indeed for some of its small seaside settlements, Crystal River or Yankeetown or Tavernier, the change is astounding — manufactured-home "communities," fast food franchises, strip shopping centers. Prepackaged living has arrived.

In the oak hammocks and orange groves, life was a simple proposition: You nestled your house under the trees or near the stream, shaded its windows with a gently sloping roof. For warmth there was the sun; for coolness, the breezes.

Often, there wasn't much to it. Most cracker settlements were little more than tumbledown shacks and tin-roofed shanties, but it would be a mistake to

Despite growth and development around it, Cross Creek still reflects serenity.

dismiss them for that: They are fine and important works of architecture, buildings of exceptional dignity and integrity.

We can still find the vestiges of a century of settlement, the few remnants that have not been trampled by our rush to develop. There still are towns so untouched that they seem almost a fabrication — towns that have witnessed this century so far without visible change. But every day more of this heritage disappears.

Such places should be precious to us for the lessons they offer; instead, they are fodder for exploitation. Today the isolated world of the Florida pioneer is a developer's dream. From Delray to Dunnellon, latter-day cracker houses grow in rows, as if they were a corn crop — clumsy, repetitive, trivialized boxes.

Architecture at its best has a sense of proportion, of harmony with the landscape. And nowhere is that more true than at Cross Creek.

At the peak of the movie-induced popularity, Alachua County's planners proposed a scheme that would make Cross Creek into a protected rural village, limiting development. Two groups of local protesters emerged — one wishing the plan more stringent, the other wanting it to be more liberal.

The public hue and cry caused Owens Illinois to put its ambitious plans on hold; its land is now on the state's ever-growing list of endangered lands in need of public acquisition.

Ultimately, Alachua County's land-use plan protected Cross Creek "from bend to bend" of the stream, restricting development right along the creek, where the Rawlings house and the fish camps are. The county now faces three lawsuits from large Cross Creek landholders.

Only one subdivision sign remains: "Creekwood, New Homes from $54,900." The dirt driveway by the sign ends in a rutted cul-de-sac; there are no new homes — yet.

And so Marjorie Kinnan Rawlings' "small place of enchantment" is secure for the moment; the protectors of the land and its buildings are in control. But at Cross Creek, the saga continues.

"Who owns Cross Creek?" asked Rawlings in the closing essay of her 1942 book of the same title. "The redbirds, I think, more than I. . . . But what of the land? It seems to me that the earth may be borrowed and not bought. It may be used and not owned. . . . We are tenants and not possessors, lovers and not masters. Cross Creek belongs to the wind and the rain, to the sun and the seasons, to the cosmic secrecy of seed, and beyond all, to time."

She didn't mention the subdividers.

The church still stands at Manatee Historical Park in Bradenton, but no one attends services. Park Director Cathy Slusser keeps watch.

8

Historical Sideshows

Buildings have been carted off and put on display as if they were zoo attractions.

Out by the Pinellas County Agricultural Extension Office is a final resting place like few others. It is called Pinellas Heritage Park, a last stop for some lovely old buildings that were uprooted by highways, houses, high-rise apartments.

Every so often, when our historic buildings get in the way of progress, we move them. We load them on barges and float them downstream, hoist them onto trucks and haul them across town.

One of the pioneer houses of Fort Lauderdale, the 1902 King-Cromartie House, was in the way of urban renewal, so it was sent upriver to a spot in Himmarshee Village near other historic buildings. Miami's oldest house, William Wagner's, was in the path of

the Metrorail, so it was transported to Lummus Park. The Brown House (1916) stood where a Holiday Inn was to go, so it was taken to Watson Island. On the way, a wing of the house crashed to the pavement on the causeway, and it has yet to be put back together.

At Pinellas Heritage Park, 14 such structures dating from 1850 to the turn of the century were given permanent repose on 22 acres of flat and shaded land midway between St. Petersburg and Clearwater in the town of Largo.

In Bradenton, the Manatee Historical Park is home to three historic buildings, including the county's first courthouse, completed in 1860 two blocks away from the grassy lawn where it now sits protected by a chain-link fence. An Episcopal church, built in 1887 and moved there in 1975 when its old location was bought by Methodists, represents the oldest religious congregation in Southwest Florida. Since the historical park is closed on Sunday mornings, there's no church service there any more.

The Pinellas Heritage Park has a Methodist church, but inside there are folding chairs and tables; its use is secular now and certainly of another era.

Most of the other buildings have furnishings more in keeping with the times in which they were built; every half hour, volunteer guides wearing long skirts and high-necked blouses show visitors around the two premier attractions, restored Victorian homes.

Jim Witherspoon serves as a guide at the Pinellas Heritage Park in Largo.

At Pinellas Heritage Park, history is repackaged so it can be taken in during a quick tour; the buildings are arrayed along brick walkways or pine-needle paths. Many of the offerings are roped off to prevent damage.

It is all very sterile, without even the spurious but entertaining flourishes of, say, restored Williamsburg, Va., where people re-enact the days of yore. Architecture and history are treated as sideshows at Pinellas Heritage Park, when at least they should be the main event.

Of course, we should be grateful that some of these buildings have been saved at all, but the price is a steep one. To put buildings on display as if they were attractions at a zoo, then to let us touch them under supervision, misses the point. It is bad enough to cage an ostrich or an antelope so we can ogle exotic animals. Presenting our own past this way is an insult.

Cities evolve slowly, and they are complex entities: To pluck a church or a train station out of its setting and then plop it down in a field without any sense of the orderly arrangement of a town lets us learn little from it. Our buildings are not part of a tabletop train set; cities don't come with interchangeable parts.

This isn't to disregard the charm of the buildings at Pinellas Heritage Park — or in any of the other architectural petting zoos in Florida or Texas or Arizona or elsewhere, for this state is not alone in this practice. They are delightful old buildings. Why else go to the expense of moving them?

Of course, there is a flip side to this as well.

In St. Augustine's restoration area is San Augustin Antiguo, billed as an "authentically restored 18th century Spanish colonial neighborhood." It is in fact something else — nine facsimiles of buildings from the 1740s and one genuine restoration, if you don't count the central air-conditioning or mind the guided tours and audio-visual presentations every half hour.

Some real 19th century buildings were torn down to make way for the blacksmith shop, the soldiers' homes and the gift shop, itself a reconstruction of a house from St. Augustine's second Spanish occupation, between 1784 and 1821.

St. Augustine is a city with a rich and varied heritage, but it is much more a product of the 19th century than the 18th century or before. Yet we have long been fixated on its Spanish past, more than any other part of the city's history. In the 1870s, Henry Flagler sent his young architects, John Carrere and Thomas Hastings, off to tour Spain before they began to design his hotels. The two architects designed the Ponce de Leon and the Alcazar in a swaggering, flamboyant Spanish style that could never have been produced during a territorial occupation.

In a way though, that sealed the city's fate, somehow diminishing the worthiness of St. Augustine's gloriously lovely late 19th and early 20th century neighborhoods, giving the city license to fabricate what it considered a more significant past, bypassing reality.

In Florida, the impulse to fiddle with history seems irresistible: If it can be moved, changed, rebuilt, reinvented, so much the better. This is, after all, a state where the main Main Street is in Disney World rather than in an actual old town.

Miami's Freedom Tower, important politically and architecturally, stands empty against a modern skyline.

9
Languishing Landmarks

Once-glorious architectural masterpieces have become nagging reminders of our disrespect.

It was an audacious time, between the Civil War and the Depression — an era of expansion, extravagance and energy.

In America, we were sure our grandest illusions could come true. We lavished love on our cities, turning bold plans into tangible realities — parks, buildings, monuments.

We built railroads and gave them stations worthy of European monarchy; we carved the states into counties, then constructed courthouses more imposing than many capitols; we planned magnificent cities adorned with broad boulevards and majestic buildings.

Historians call this period of architecture the American Renaissance, its credo uttered by the architect Daniel Burnham: "Make no little plans."

In Florida, no scheme was too daring, no monument too immense. The object was beauty, of course, but if fame and glory came to our cities as well, that was fine, too.

Thus, in Lakeland a vast chimerical promenade with surrealistic pavilions studded with Corinthian columns was placed around Lake Mirror as the city's crowning glory.

In Daytona Beach, the expansive beach was adorned with a sprawling stone pavilion with a clock tower and a handsome band shell.

In DeFuniak Springs, a lake became the focal point

Times have changed for this old clock in Daytona Beach.

for a remarkable cupola-topped building, the Chautauqua Auditorium. In Bartow and Blountstown, Madison and Monticello, the courthouses harked back to the architecture of Thomas Jefferson.

In Coral Gables, every detail, down to the fountains and plazas and gateways, was drawn to give it an other-worldly character. In Venice, a visionary plan ensured the city's elegance; in Avon Park, the main street was made resplendent by thousands of flowering trees.

But our romance with our cities has waned over the years, and they are no longer the heroic places we once thought they might become. They are too dirty, too dangerous, too drab. We don't tend them, nurture them, adorn them the way we once did.

Our civic monuments have become decrepit eyesores. Once-glorious architectural masterpieces have become nagging reminders of our disrespect. Across Florida, we have let some of our most important landmarks languish.

Surrealistic columns on the walk around Lake Mirror once made a spectacular centerpiece for the city of Lakeland.

When Ohio Gov. James Cox wanted a home for his *Miami Daily News,* nothing less than a rendition of the most beautiful building in Seville, the Giralda, would do; its lyrical lines would give it an almost magical appearance against the deep blue Miami sky.

Eventually, the newspaper moved out, and the building became a processing center for the Cubans who came to Miami in the '60s and '70s. It got a new name, the Freedom Tower, and it earned political and emotional importance in the city, as well as architectural. Then it was abandoned.

The Freedom Tower is a symbol of hope and of helplessness — a landmark decaying before our eyes. In the skyline, its magic endures. But up close, the Freedom Tower is much defiled. For years, it has been neglected. For years, futures worthy of its past have been discussed — municipal offices, a hotel, a university building — and never carried out.

It is a great frustration.

And there are many others.

DeFuniak Springs' Chautauqua Auditorium dates back to 1885; it was the second meeting house in the country built by utopian dreamers; the first was in western New York. Today that fragile wood building is the headquarters of Walton County's Chamber of Commerce, and it has suffered. Ceilings have been dropped, floors covered over with indoor-outdoor carpeting, and the building is in general disrepair.

Daytona Beach's gorgeous beachfront pavilion should be a showplace, but it isn't. It is sparsely landscaped, its magnificence too little appreciated.

True, the band shell is spruced up with pink and sea-green paint, a nice nod to the pavilion's grace and its 60-year history. But the pavilion is dotted with benches covered with ads for pizza parlors and country-and-western bars, its striking design further diminished by tasteless trash cans and phone booths. The bathhouse is festooned with a tacky plastic sign with red and blue letters.

This is not a matter of mere subtleties. This beachfront pavilion is truly wonderful: In Florida, there is nothing else like it. It ought to be Daytona Beach's signature structure, but it isn't.

When it was completed in 1926, the Lake Mirror Promenade was Lakeland's proudest achievement. Postcards depicted it as if it were a painting by El Greco — moonlit, alluring, almost eerie.

But the triumphs of another era fade for us; one generation's accomplishment is scorned by another. The Lake Mirror Promenade has been misused, abused, misunderstood.

Traffic now rushes by the promenade where no roads used to go. The idyllic view is shared by a dry cleaner, a feed store, a gas station, a bus depot.

The promenade itself, originally a wide walkway encircling the lake, is now a narrow path, shaved away to make room for the road around it. In some spots it is inaccessible, in others it has been reduced to rubble. The huge, freestanding acanthus-topped columns are chipped in spots; many of the light fixtures are missing.

Yet it is easy to look at the Lake Mirror Promenade and envision it elegant, with gardens and paddle boats and music; off on one side are two of Lakeland's old hotels and its palazzo-like City Hall. Preliminary plans for restoration are under way, and if we're lucky, Lake Mirror may someday be a gala place again. Even today, the promenade and its lake are so enthralling that it matters less that the water is stagnant.

Looking along the Lakeland Promenade.

But still it *is* stagnant, and that tells us something about how little we care about our landmarks.

Of course, we built our parks or plazas or civic monuments for narcissistic reasons, to aggrandize our cities, but we also built them for the greater good. In days past, municipal pride was reason enough.

But that is an elusive quality: Pride doesn't necessarily show up in election polls, nor can it be quantified by financial analysts.

There are some misplaced priorities at work here: Cities all over Florida work hard at their own public relations: Daytona boasts of its funky "strip," Miami of its cosmopolitan downtown.

So we let the paint peel and the timbers rot while the graffiti artists have their way. And then we wonder why we don't feel better about where we live.

Paul Rudolph's Sarasota High School has been emblazoned with Halloween colors; its original architectural intent is obscured.
Photograph courtesy of Sarasota Historical Society.

10

Four Architects – Legacies Misunderstood

We have sacrificed art for expediency, be it bureaucratic or economic, and in so doing we have jeopardized some of our finest works by architects like Mizner, Rudolph, Wright and Klutho.

Paul Rudolph, one of the most important modern architects in America, lived in Sarasota in the decade after World War II. There, he designed beach houses and high schools that were a thrilling sight — spare and graceful and elegant.

Soon, connoisseurs of architecture from all over the world were making pilgrimages to look at what Rudolph had wrought.

The buildings were breathtakingly beautiful, structures with daring swoops to their roofs and precipitous positions right at the water's edge. For their stark modernity, they had a remarkable delicacy: Fragile latticework screening, slender columns, sun-dappled courtyards made them seem somehow diaphanous.

Rudolph was among the first in America to put

to work the ideas of the Bauhaus, and when he did it in Sarasota it was clear that a genius was at the drawing board.

But today, his brilliant achievements there are anything but celebrated. Only a few structures have been well cared for; and they only underscore the tragedy of the others.

The others sport coats of paint in cloying colors, stand next to new additions of clumsy styling and proportion. Some of them, houses especially, have been dramatically altered; others — and his two high schools are the case in point here — bear the scars of almost three decades of reckless occupancy and bullheaded bureaucracy.

Great architecture is great art, and yet we feel free to

Henry John Klutho of Jacksonville was Florida's premier Prairie School architect. His St. James Building, his masterpiece, has been much changed. Photograph courtesy of Florida State Archives.

ruin it. To spray-paint a Picasso or slash a Rembrandt is a crime; the same is not true of even the work of our most sacred architects — Frank Lloyd Wright, H.H. Richardson, Thomas Jefferson.

In Florida, we have destroyed architectural masterpieces with impunity. The state's foremost Prairie School architect, Henry John Klutho, completed one of his best works in 1913, the St. James Building in Jacksonville. Domed and skylighted, it had intricate detailing and magnificent proportions. Today, as May-Cohen's Department Store, it is substantially changed outside, drastically different inside — ''marred on the exterior and completely lost within,'' said architect and Klutho scholar Robert Broward. Even the skylit dome has been closed in.

Just this summer, the Palm Beach Town Council

approved the removal of a staircase from the Via Mizner, the staircase to Addison Mizner's own apartment and studio, which he called the Villa Mizner. For years, Villa Mizner remained a private residence with shops on the ground floor; now, while alterations are being made to the building, it is being used as offices.

Mizner built it in 1924 and moved in along with his dogs, cats, birds and monkeys. Historian Donald Curl wrote of Mizner's afternoons at home there during which the architect had string quartets entertain or merely told stories of his own society exploits; up on the fifth floor, he designed the wonderful structures that made Palm Beach so picturesque.

Mizner was clearly the most illustrious architect of the era; his home and studio should be a shrine, a study center or a reading room perhaps — not just a piece of another commercial venture.

Frank Lloyd Wright designed nine buildings for the Florida Southern College campus in Lakeland; he set them gracefully amid a spectacular orange grove, and linked them with a series of stunning breezeways. He studded his windows with chips of stained glass and trimmed his roofs in copper.

The orange grove is long gone, but the buildings remain. They make up the largest congregation of Wright buildings in America, yet they are given little of their due. New buildings, considerably less striking, surround Wright's. At Florida Southern, tight budgets mean patching up rather than maintaining, painting bogus copper trim rather than replacing the metal.

When he first came to Florida, Rudolph spent his Sundays driving out to see Wright's work at Florida Southern, and its geometry and subtlety were a certain influence. Wright spoke of Florida in glowing superlatives; he saw in the vast blue skies and lush green landscape the potential for creating buildings that were peculiar to this one special place.

Rudolph followed suit. His architecture was definitely of Florida, buildings that blended easily into Siesta Key's scrub or sat gently among mainland Sarasota's Australian pines. For the most part, they

The vias Addison Mizner designed as alleys and courtyards off Worth Avenue were evocative of another world. He chose to live in his own villa overlooking the Via Mizner; now its architecture has been altered. Photograph courtesy of Florida State Archives.

needed no air-conditioning, relying instead on complex circulation systems that let the breezes flow. Sunlight shone through huge picture windows and narrow clerestories, through lattices and light wells; but there were also broad overhangs — decorative canopies or, even more appealing, movable fins and louvers known as *brise soleils* — to ensure that the light was always indirect.

Look today at Riverview High School and it is clear that Rudolph's message has been too long misunderstood. Once-airy corridors have become dark tunnels; skylights have been covered over with plywood or concrete or merely blocked by air-conditioning ducts. "They were just shoved in," said Carl Abbott, an award-winning architect who chose to settle in Sarasota because Rudolph, his dean at Yale, had worked there during the '50s.

At Sarasota High School, the school colors of orange and black have been emblazoned everywhere as if a Halloween prankster had gone berserk. Where once there were windows, now there is blank wall. A soaring two-story cafeteria was cut in half horizontally. The intended approach to the school has been obstructed by untended overgrowth and a chain-link fence, so it is impossible to see it as it was designed.

Both schools should be cherished by school administrators as precious landmarks. Yet they bear the signs of our times — graffiti, vandalism, chipped paint, dirt.

We have sacrificed art for expediency, be it bureaucratic or economic, and in so doing we have jeopardized some of our finest works of architecture.

I have seen the Villa Mizner a hundred times at least, the Florida Southern campus a half-dozen. I have seen Riverview High School only once. Each takes my breath away, every time. That is great architecture's continuing power. Despite all the damage that has been done over the years, these buildings have a compelling, even hypnotic, presence.

It is sad testimony to our values that such brilliant architecture has been treated so thoughtlessly, kept so carelessly. We are privileged to have such buildings, and we have abused that privilege.

Frank Lloyd Wright's Florida Southern College buildings comprise the largest collection of his work in one place. Over the years, the buildings have suffered a bit. Photograph courtesy of Florida State Archives.

Developers are finding profit in restoring the Art Deco District's delightful stucco hotels and apartment buildings.

11

"Real Florida" Beware

Florida is being divided up, patched together and put on the market, ready for the next onslaught of population.

From the tip of Key West to the top of the Panhandle, from fragile coastal villages to sweet small towns, the future is at hand and the past is fast disappearing.

We are losing the battle of history. Grand hotels stand empty, with no future but dereliction. Hidden-away houses are just as endangered as prominent downtown landmarks. Quiet fishing communities are becoming bustling commercial enterprises — havens for condo dwellers and chic shoppers.

All over Florida, growth and change are inevitable. Statistics tell us how rapid the growth rate is: Florida has six of the nation's ten fastest-growing municipalities. Measuring change is somewhat harder, except after the fact.

Yet on U.S. 19 north of New Port Richey it is possible to see what Florida is becoming everywhere — an incessant cacophony of strip shopping centers and signs, bowling alleys, supermarkets, drug stores, discount stores all sitting behind vast asphalt parking lots.

Roads across the state are littered with billboards, advertising $100-down subdivisions, retirement communities and mobile home parks.

"The Real Florida," announces one series of billboards, trying to lure people to a huge and arid development called Citrus Springs, a place prophetically devoid of most of Florida's redeeming charms. That is the "Real Florida" as we will come to know it if we don't watch out.

Of course, there has always been growth to contend with, roughly from 1822, the year Florida became an American territory and settlement began in earnest. But for the first century and a half, the people who built Florida still thought it was a special place, and they rejoiced in its potential for romance and entrancement.

Thus whole cities were created in a picture-book image of an American "Riviera," and hotels with the massing and presence of a Spanish castle or an Italian palazzo. Thus shipping ports with demure cottages and proud, ornate houses; pioneer settlements with structures so simple and scenic that they almost merge with the glorious landscape.

In the face of all the converging forces that prey on our historic architecture — demolition, neglect, exploitation among them — we stand a chance of losing much too much of it.

Next onslaught?

Time is not on our side. Florida is being divided up, patched together and put on the market, ready for the next onslaught of population. Look around on any morning anywhere in the state.

On a country lane north of DeLand in northeast Florida, the surveyors are at work. The drive is punctuated by For Sale signs. Once, this road led to a pleasant old hotel at a cool, clear spring. Now all that is left of the past at DeLeon State Park is an old Spanish sugar mill, and even its future is up in the air.

On Estero Island off Fort Myers, a crew works to rebuild the dune in front of the Beacon Motel. Next door, the seawall is painted blue to warn passersby that there is "no trespassing." The concrete wall is inches from the water, though it is not yet high tide.

A fierce rainstorm drums down on Aripeka, a tiny Gulf Coast village hemmed in by new development. At the center of the town are some old unpainted shacks and a hand-scrawled sign that tells us, perhaps apocryphally, that Hernando DeSoto, Winslow Homer, Orville and Wilbur Wright, Babe Ruth and Jack Dempsey were among those who passed through.

There is another sign, too. It says: "For Sale, By Owner." The asking price: $370,000.

A lot of our history is on the auction block these days — from grand mansions to humble cottages.

There is profit in preservation, and that is a mixed blessing. In the case of the property in Aripeka, where 4.5 acres zoned for commercial use encircle the rundown fishing shacks, the profit comes from exploiting the quaint, the legendary or the beautiful.

But investors can be persuaded that their interest and the public interest can coincide when old buildings are saved, as is happening these days in Miami Beach where developers are finding profit in restoring the Art Deco District's delightful stucco hotels and apartment buildings.

Developers will continue to invest in historic buildings as long as there are tax credits for such renovation, although every year those benefits are in jeopardy of being eliminated.

Two decades have passed since the U.S. Congress wrote the National Historic Preservation Act, which the state's top preservation officer, George Percy, regards as the single most important step we have taken toward salvaging pieces of our past. That act established a national program of historic preservation and encouraged the listing of buildings on the National Register of Historic Places.

By now, Florida has enrolled 549 structures and districts on the register. But in some places in the state, only the most obvious historic buildings are on the list. In Santa Rosa County, home to the lovely side-by-side towns of Milton and Bagdad where history is rapidly being encroached upon by commercial development, only one place has made it to the register: St. Mary's Episcopal Church and Rectory.

Too, the National Register is entirely voluntary, so there are huge gaps on its rolls: Miami's William Vanderbilt mansion isn't listed, nor is the Chinsegut Hill house that is the University of South Florida's conference center. In Florida there are 15 counties where no buildings at all have been nominated to the National Register.

Just one tool

The National Register is just one tool for recognizing the worth of historic properties. The best protection against the wrecking ball is local legislation, either zoning codes or preservation ordinances.

Yet two of Florida's largest cities, Tampa and Jacksonville, have no preservation ordinances. St.

Petersburg, one of the state's great treasure troves of early 20th century buildings, just got its preservation law this year.

And in the face of a fervent desire to demolish, the local laws cannot finally banish the bulldozer; the best we can do is delay the inevitable. For example, Miami's excellent heritage conservation ordinance couldn't save Gesu School, the city's oldest Catholic school.

In far too many Florida cities and counties, the demolitionists and the developers have the elected officials' ears, by dint of persuasion, pocketbook or both. The biggest task is persuading the politicians that it is better to preserve than destroy.

In Evinston, the old post office stands as a reminder of an era past.

It can be done. Just last month, Miami Beach designated its first two local historic districts within the national Art Deco District; it was the first municipal acknowledgment of the architectural treasures stored in that mile-square area, but even that was hard-earned. Citizens packed City Hall in enough numbers to convince commissioners to vote in the public interest rather than with the private developers who opposed the historic designation.

The past has its avid protectors in Florida, from the state's Percy and his staff, to preservation boards and city planners across the state down to the general public.

The Florida Trust for Historic Preservation, a private, nonprofit organization, has acquired its first property, the lovely Bonnet House in Fort Lauderdale. It is moving ahead with other programs including a revolving fund intended to save historic buildings that have no other angels: The first of these are four Victorian houses on University Avenue in Gainesville.

The state's Historic Preservation Division was further empowered last year with an amended law (the first was passed 13 years ago) that strengthens its man-date. This year, too, the division is at work on an updated statewide preservation plan that addresses the future squarely, laying out the issues and outlining the tasks ahead. Even in draft form it is a good plan, for it reflects the seriousness of the situation.

We have sometimes been too willing to categorize, and in so doing, we can obscure the real issues. Often a fine line divides what is architecturally or historically important from what is environmentally significant. When the last beachfront cottage goes to make way for a high-rise, it is safe to assume that the beach is in danger too.

A case in point is the Florida Keys where the Monroe County Land Use Plan looks at how to build in the future more than how to save what is already there.

We've always regarded the protection of the Keys as an environmental issue when there are questions of architecture and historic preservation as well.

We must take steps to protect our town squares and city parks as architectural resources, so that such exquisite green spaces as Ocala's town square are not simply paved over for parking or plowed up for high-rise development. The old guidebooks praise Florida's tropical gardens, and we have few of those left: We must strive not to lose them, even to neglect. We have come near to obliterating the Japanese Garden on Miami's Watson Island that way.

We also must deal better with the recent past. Somehow, buildings and artifacts that we know *will be* important to history nonetheless seem to stump us.

In Florida, we must continue to broaden our definition of what is historic, so that we do not wipe out the last of our unassuming villages or tear down elegant old neighborhoods or destroy our wonderful rural roadways. We must begin to regard our historic buildings and neighborhoods with the same reverence we bestow on our finest museums, for that is what they are.

Splendid and simple

Home movies show me the Florida I first knew as a young visitor — those giddy, ridiculous moving pictures of my family in front of unpretentious beach-front motels or a tiny one-story house overwhelmed by the banyan tree out front. Our winter trips to escape the bitter cold of the Cleveland suburbs took us to Florida a dozen times or so between 1950 and 1970.

These places stick in my childhood memory: Bok Tower, Bahia Mar, Cypress Gardens, Key West, Vizcaya, Wolfie's, Webb City. I remember the splendid and the simple in equal proportion, and still today, I believe that is what Florida is all about.

In the end, the past is personal, and that is what makes preserving it so urgent. It is our own memories intermingled with a collective memory that we call history; it is not truth so much as interpretation, but in that interpretation we can find beauty and wisdom, inspiration for living and guidance for the future.

But most of all in the past we find what human beings crave — continuity, the linkages that hold generation to generation, parent to child.

My son will graduate from high school in the year 2001. I hope I will be able to show him some of the Florida that I knew as a child, or even the Florida that I knew as an adult. I may have to do that quickly, before it vanishes.

Florida embraces growth and change; its history is being eradicated.

Update

Since the original publication of these essays in the *Miami Herald* in July and August of 1986, some changes have occurred. The Biscaya Hotel in Miami Beach was demolished. The Ormond Hotel went into foreclosure and faces an uncertain fate. The John Ringling Towers in Sarasota is being renovated. The Chautauqua building in DeFuniak Springs has been partially renovated, also. The roof over the Vizcaya courtyard is completed. This is, of course, only a partial list.

All the buildings and communities mentioned here remain subject to the vagaries of Florida's unparalleled development. By some statisticians' count, Florida has just become the fourth most populous state. The rate of population increase is exceeding almost all expectations. It is now forecast that 12.6 million people will be living in Florida by 1990.

Index